ESSENTIAL  MANAGERS

MANAGING PEOPLE

ROBERT HELLER

DK PUBLISHING, INC.

A DK PUBLISHING BOOK
www.dk.com

Produced for Dorling Kindersley
by Cooling Brown

Editor Jane Cooke
Designer Juliette Norsworthy
Creative Director Arthur Brown

DTP Designer Jason Little
Production Controller Silvia La Greca

Series Editor Adèle Hayward
Series Art Editor Tassy King
US Editors Gary Werner, Chuck Wills
Managing Editors Stephanie Jackson,
Jonathan Metcalf
Managing Art Editor Nigel Duffield

First American Edition, 1999
6 8 10 9 7 5

Published in the United States by
DK Publishing, Inc.
95 Madison Avenue, New York, New York 10016

DK Publishing books are available at special discounts for
bulk purchases for sales promotions or premiums. Special
editions, including personalized covers, excerpts of existing
guides, and corporate imprints can be created in large
quantities for specific needs. For more information, contact
Special Markets Dept./DK Publishing, Inc./95 Madison
Ave./New York, New York 10016/Fax: 800-600-9098.

Library of Congress Cataloging-in-Publication Data

Heller, Robert, 1932–
Managing People / by Robert Heller --
1st American ed.
p. cm. -- (Essential managers)
Includes index.
ISBN 0-7894-4861-0 (alk.paper)
1. Psychology, Industrial. 2. Supervision of
employees. 3. Management. 4. Interpersonal
relations. 5. Job stress – Prevention.
I. Title. II. Series.
HF5548.8.H377 1999
158.7--dc21   99-15777
                                              CIP

Reproduced by Colourscan, Singapore
Printed in Hong Kong by Wing King Tong Co. Ltd.

CONTENTS

4 INTRODUCTION

DEVELOPING BASIC PEOPLE SKILLS

6 UNDERSTANDING BEHAVIOR

8 UNDERSTANDING PEOPLE'S NEEDS

10 LEARNING THE BASICS

12 BUILDING CONFIDENCE

14 COMMUNICATING CLEARLY

18 GAINING TRUST AND COMMITMENT

22 ADJUSTING YOUR APPROACH

DEVELOPING PEOPLE

24 PROVIDING TRAINING

26 IMPROVING SKILLS

28 GUIDING OTHERS

30 TEACHING BY EXAMPLE

32 NURTURING TALENT

34 ENCOURAGING MANAGEMENT POTENTIAL

36 MOTIVATING PEOPLE

38 IMPROVING PERFORMANCE

40 MAKING PROGRESS

FINDING SOLUTIONS

42 BUILDING ENVIRONMENTS

44 OPENING CLOSED MINDS

46 DEALING WITH CONFLICT

48 WORKING COLLECTIVELY

50 DEALING WITH PERSONAL DIFFICULTIES

52 MANAGING CHANGE

ASSESSING AND REWARDING

54 EVALUATING PERFORMANCE

56 PROMOTING STAFF

58 TURNING FAILURE INTO SUCCESS

60 REMUNERATING EFFECTIVELY

62 USING INCENTIVES

64 CREATING PARTNERSHIPS

66 ASSESSING YOUR ABILITY

70 INDEX

72 ACKNOWLEDGMENTS

INTRODUCTION

Today's fast-moving business environment demands that the effective manager be both a well-organized administrator and highly adept in understanding people's basic needs and behavior in the workplace. Gaining commitment, nurturing talent, and ensuring that people are motivated and productive requires open communication and trust between managers and staff. Managing People will help you to master the fundamentals of successful management techniques that will enable you to get the best out of the people who work for you. It also demonstrates how, by identifying and avoiding common problems, managers can turn potential failure into success for their organization. A wealth of practical advice is supplemented by 101 useful tips and a comprehensive self-assessment exercise.

DEVELOPING BASIC PEOPLE SKILLS

Knowing why people behave as they do is the key to gaining their commitment. Aim to understand people's needs in order to motivate them and thus meet the demands of the organization.

UNDERSTANDING BEHAVIOR

Natural, instinctive behavior is not always appropriate in the workplace. Make an effort to produce behavioral patterns that lead to productive and effective teamwork in your employees.

BEHAVING NATURALLY

People at work naturally tend to adopt instinctive modes of behavior that are self-protective rather than open and collaborative. This explains why emotion is a strong force in the workplace, and why management often reacts fiercely to criticism and usually seeks to control rather than take risks. People also tend to leap to conclusions and fragment into small, often warring, groups. Companies exhibiting "natural" behavior like this are highly political and emphasize status and hierarchy. They are less pleasant to work for and generally at odds with the needs of people and the marketplace.

▲ ENCOURAGING
CONSTRUCTIVENESS
You can encourage constructive attitudes in people most effectively by example and reward, and by always approving of their good conduct and positive contributions.

BEHAVING APPROPRIATELY

Natural behavior is based on subjective responses that can often lead not only to negative feelings (such as insecurity), but also to mistaken perceptions concerning the intentions of other staff members. More constructive behavioral attributes will encourage cooperation, openness, and self-confidence. Some readily recognizable traits of people with appropriate behavioral skills include a proven facility to communicate positively and confidently with colleagues at all levels; the swift and generous recognition of the achievements of others; the ability to learn from mistakes and failures; and a general approach that is based on collaboration with fellow workers rather than competition.

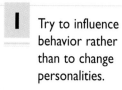

1 Try to influence behavior rather than to change personalities.

2 Encourage and reward constructive behavior.

REPLACING NEGATIVE CHARACTERISTICS

NATURAL BEHAVIOR

- Reacting emotionally when information is received.
- Avoiding risks through fear or insecurity.
- Fighting fiercely and defensively when under threat.
- Making snap judgments about people and events.
- Spreading gossip throughout the organization.
- Competing for status and its symbols.
- Dwelling on past successes.
- Feeling more comfortable in small factions.
- Always seeking hierarchical superiority.

APPROPRIATE BEHAVIOR

- Establishing the facts using a pragmatic approach.
- Taking risks in an entrepreneurial fashion.
- Forming collegiate, collaborative, non-combative relationships.
- Insisting on detailed analysis before judgment.
- Practicing totally open communication.
- Recognizing achievement, not status.
- Learning from mistakes.
- Choosing to work in cooperative groups.
- Operating within flat, non-hierarchical structures.

UNDERSTANDING PEOPLE'S NEEDS

People's needs go far beyond basics, such as good working conditions and fair pay. But you cannot meet people's higher needs, such as pride in work and sharing in the corporate goals, without addressing basics.

3 Take care that people's lower-level needs are met.

▼ **PRIORITIZING NEEDS**

The psychologist Abraham Maslow has identified a five-stage "hierarchy of needs," starting with basic needs for food and shelter, and culminating in higher-level "self-actualization," or self-fulfillment, needs.

MEETING NEEDS

People have various kinds of needs. Examples of lower-level needs are salary, job security, and working conditions. You have to meet these basic needs, but doing so will not by itself give satisfaction. Failures with the basic needs nearly always explain dissatisfaction among staff. Satisfaction, on the other hand, springs from meeting higher-level needs, such as responsibility, progress, and personal growth.

3) Social needs are fulfilled by friendly interaction with other people

2) Secondary needs are for personal security

4) Higher-level esteem needs are met by recognition of achievements

1) Basic needs are for food, shelter, and warmth

5) Self-actualization needs are realized by achieving total individual potential

ENCOURAGING PRIDE

People need to feel that their contribution is valued and unique. Pride in work has two forms: individual and collective. If you work on an assembly line, for example, you are pleased with your own performance at, say, installing a car door. But you are also proud of the whole car to which you have contributed. As a manager, seek to exploit this pride in others, and be proud of your own ability to handle staff with positive results. Both management and staff should feel proud to belong to an admired company.

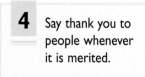

4 Say thank you to people whenever it is merited.

5 Add public praise to private words to raise pride.

IDENTIFYING SOURCES OF SATISFACTION

LOWER-LEVEL NEEDS

CONDITIONS
Reasonable hours, a pleasant environment, and adequate equipment: "I approve of the physical working conditions."

SUPERVISION
Empowerment and encouragement given by immediate managers: "I like the way I am treated by those who supervise me."

SECURITY
Confidence in the organization's outlook and a feeling of belonging: "I feel good about the future of the organization."

MANAGEMENT
An understanding of management methods: "I think the organization is making the changes necessary to be competitive."

COMMUNICATION
Full awareness of the organization's plans and involvement in the planning: "I understand and identify with the organization's strategy."

HIGHER-LEVEL NEEDS

JOB INTEREST
Satisfaction derived from the actual job content and its execution: "I like the kind of work that I do."

ACHIEVEMENT
Motivation to hit targets and to perform tasks at high levels of effectiveness: "My work gives me a sense of accomplishment."

COMMITMENT
Pleasure through belonging to the organization and identifying with it: "I am proud to say I work for the organization."

RESPONSIBILITY
Work requirements that stretch the individual, but are fair and rewarding: "I welcome the amount of work I am expected to do."

IDENTIFICATION
People understand how they fit into the overall plan: "I see how my work connects with the organization's strategies."

LEARNING THE BASICS

To understand people's attitudes, you need to be open to all the ways in which they communicate. Learn to listen to what they say – and do not say – and look out for other signals, such as body language.

> **6** Ask open questions that encourage total honesty.

LISTENING CAREFULLY

In many areas of a manager's job, from meetings and appraisals to telephone calls, listening plays a key role. Listening benefits both you and your staff: you gain a greater insight into people and potentially receive useful ideas about how your organization can be improved, while staff feel their views are being heard and will therefore respond more openly. Consider how you listen: do you interrupt frequently or cut people short to make your point? If so, practice remaining quiet and concentrating on the speaker; if necessary ask brief questions to ensure you have understood what they are saying. If you are easily distracted, practice focusing on the speaker's words, repeating key phrases silently to fix them in your mind. As well as actually hearing what a person says, you need to look and behave as if you are listening, for example, by appearing relaxed and open and nodding frequently.

> **7** Give people ample opportunity to express their true feelings.

Employee expresses true feelings

**DISCUSSING ▶
OPENLY**
Make an effort to understand people's attitudes by careful listening and questioning, and by giving them the opportunity to express themselves.

INTERPRETING CORRECTLY

Listen to what a person says, and then mentally review their words to check you have understood their meaning. If you have not, ask them to clarify what they have said. You can also rephrase what they have said and repeat it back to them, giving them a chance to agree with or correct your statement. Look at the whole meaning of what a person is saying rather than selecting the parts you want to hear. Always take what you are told on trust, unless you have good reason not to. If the person is contradicting themselves or being evasive, they may not be telling the whole story, so continue questioning until you are satisfied.

8 Keep asking questions until you understand what someone means.

9 Practice reading people's body language.

READING BODY LANGUAGE

Manager encourages an open response by listening and asking affirming questions

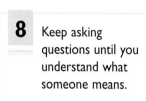

Body language is the term for the unconscious physical movements we all make that communicate thoughts and feelings. Interpreting body language correctly is a complex art, but you can easily learn to read broad messages. An open, relaxed posture and good eye contact are indications that a person is comfortable with themselves and what they are saying or hearing. A tense posture, perhaps with arms crossed and little eye contact, may indicate evasiveness, suppressed anger, or disagreement. Leaning forward when seated may indicate interest or agreement, while leaning back indicates lack of interest or resistance. Be aware of these signals in yourself as well as in others.

BUILDING CONFIDENCE

Most people suffer from insecurity at some time. The many kinds of anxiety that affect people in organizations can feed such insecurity. Your antidote is to build confidence by giving recognition, high-level tasks, and full information.

10 Go to the rescue at once if people show that a task is beyond them.

REDUCING INSECURITY

Some people conceal their insecurity better than others, but do not be deceived. Everybody needs to be told that they are performing well and that they are respected, both for what they are and for what they have done and are doing. Praise is a very effective (and very economical) way of improving confidence, but be sure that it is deserved. Then suit the method of praise to the circumstances.

▼ **WELCOMING INPUT**
Bolster the confidence of all individuals, especially more reticent types, by allowing everyone at a meeting to speak in turn.

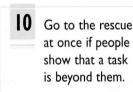

Committee leader invites input from all

Unconfident member is encouraged to speak

11 Avoid giving false reassurances – be frank if the news is not good.

ENCOURAGING ABILITY

Lack of confidence often holds people back from seeking out (or sometimes accepting) new challenges at work. Even very confident people operate at a small percentage of their maximum capacity or potential. Encourage staff to believe in their own abilities by giving them additional tasks – for instance, asking them to serve on committees tackling key issues. Do not accept the response "I'm no good at that." This is often merely an unconscious excuse for inaction.

ELIMINATING FEAR

People suffer from many kinds of fear: fear of personal failure; fear that the organization will fail or be taken over; fear that jobs will disappear through reorganization; or fear of the possible adverse consequences of change. None of these anxieties is irrational. They are only eased, though never completely eliminated, by full, frank, and open communication – with individuals and groups. The anxieties can be exacerbated by secretive management that uses fear as a way to control people. Drive out fear and you will find that trust, optimism, and kindness are much more effective.

Open, upright posture shows confidence

Withdrawn appearance shows lack of self-belief

▲ **READING BODY LANGUAGE**

The outward appearance of a person often gives insight into their feelings: An employee exhibiting defensive body language and a negative attitude may be feeling insecure.

12 Insist on people working together and communicating freely and openly.

ENABLING PARTICIPATION

Confidence in the workplace stems from true participation in the work. This can only happen when employees – singly or in groups – share information and therefore have a real influence over what actually happens. The advantages are democratic, motivational, and practical. Research shows that productivity is lower when jobs are closely prescribed, compared with situations in which people are allowed to contribute in their own ways to meeting goals.

POINTS TO REMEMBER

- Stepping back and letting others take the lead helps both you and your staff to be confident.
- Letting your own insecurity show will infect your team.
- Uncertainty always breeds low morale.
- It is important to inform people of company developments quickly and honestly.

COMMUNICATING CLEARLY

Sometimes highly organized, sometimes haphazard, communication happens all the time. Improve its quality by being open, honest, and accessible to everybody. You can never communicate too much, whether informally or formally.

13 Go out of your way to chat to staff on an informal basis.

THINGS TO DO

1. Keep appointments with all members of staff, regardless of their status.
2. Make sure you talk to or acknowledge people as often as you can.
3. On outside visits, talk to everybody, not just the boss.
4. If you want to speak with a staff member, make the effort to meet them in person rather than using the telephone.

OPEN PLANNING ▶
Open-plan offices encourage open communication and team spirit as well as making managers more accessible to staff.

14 Split large working units into several smaller ones with close links.

ENCOURAGING CONTACT

Many managers like to hide away behind closed office doors, keeping contact to a minimum. That makes it easy to be an administrator, but very hard to be a leader. It is far better to keep your office door open (as a general rule) and to encourage people to visit you when the door is open. Contact is made easier by open-plan work spaces, which is why some multimillionaire managers in Silicon Valley have abandoned their executive suites for desks in an open-plan office. If you have not talked to a particular member of staff for a while, make sure you do so. The more people who know you and can see you, the better working relationships are likely to be.

CUTTING BUREAUCRACY

If left unchecked, bureaucracy can severely impede communications, rendering attempts to improve productivity and morale ineffective. Although there is a need for some bureaucracy, it is important that you keep strict control over forms, reports, and other such documents. Avoid wasting time waiting for a proposal to be "rubber-stamped" when a decision can be taken in a quick, but effective, informal meeting.

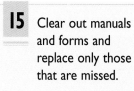

15 Clear out manuals and forms and replace only those that are missed.

CONSIDERING HOW ORGANIZATIONS COMMUNICATE

TYPE OF ORGANIZATION	EFFECTS ON COMMUNICATION
BUREAUCRATIC Dominated by hierarchies of power.	A domineering, "who reports to whom?" structure leads to rigid control, abundant manuals, systems, reports, and paperwork.
MATRIX Divided by product, geography, and function.	This type of organization is supposedly coordinated, but the leadership is divided and the bureaucracy is strong.
DECENTRALIZED Divided into separate operating units.	The individual units function separately or independently, so communication is difficult – the organization is primarily driven by budgets.
MARKET-ORIENTED Organized by product and/or geography.	A strong sales culture is dominated by commands from head office, so communication with outside staff is limited.
ENTREPRENEURIAL Flat structure with risk-taking philosophy.	The tendency to "hire-and-fire" people can lead to a culture of fear. Decisions are usually dependent on one or two key people.
PEOPLE-BASED Employees own shares and enjoy responsibility.	Staff are motivated by ownership in the company. People participate in and have responsibility for the company's management.

ONE-ON-ONE MEETINGS

Instead of relying on memos and other written communications, consider the immediacy of the one-on-one meeting as the most efficient way to deal with issues or problems that arise. Instant feedback and endorsements can be given at these personal meetings, and enthusiasm and commitment to new proposals or fresh ideas can be conveyed much more effectively and unambiguously than through written responses. Ensure that you have enough time available to give your full attention to matters under discussion, and that the meeting will not be unnecessarily interrupted or cut short.

QUESTIONS TO ASK YOURSELF

Q Has my message been well received and understood?

Q Do key customers think that I spend enough time visiting them and that my calls are productive?

Q Do I end meetings before people have had their say?

Q Do I hear rumors in enough time to dispel them?

Q Have I met everybody I should in the past week?

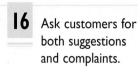

16 Ask customers for both suggestions and complaints.

USING DIFFERENT MEDIA

One channel of communication is never enough – the more there are, the better. Your objective is to pass on information as quickly as possible, and to learn, just as speedily, about reactions to your messages. Noticeboards, newsletters, and magazines all have their place, as do suggestion boxes. But electronic media are more immediate and powerful. You can use digital noticeboards, Web sites, in-company television, video, and email. The same rules apply to all media: work to professional standards, match content to employees' needs, encourage feedback, and be prepared to change the format if the presentation is ill-received. Analyze the response to ensure that your message has been fully understood and has had the effect that you intended.

Company Web site

◀ USING NEW MEDIA

The wealth of new technology available to organizations means that company communications can be made more immediately and with greater impact than ever before.

USING THE "GRAPEVINE"

People at work form social networks and interact in the same way as all human groups. They value informal contacts, such as personal greetings and chats over tea and coffee. They also gossip. Some managers distrust the grapevine and worry that inaccurate, premature, and alarming information will spread. The grapevine, though, can be fed by management with accurate "rumors." Disarm its disruptive potential with swift information on matters that concern people. Often the best way to learn what is on people's minds is through informal meetings, so make sure that you participate fully in them.

▼ **REMAINING INFORMAL**
Informal chats are a useful way of finding out how your staff feel and of discouraging rumors and gossip.

Employee discusses team problems

Manager eases concern at source

17 Act swiftly to deny rumors if they are inaccurate.

18 Ensure that all those at meetings need to be there.

USING TEAM MEETINGS

In most organizations meetings occur more often than is necessary. Ensure that every meeting has a purpose, and that all attendees are directly concerned with that purpose. Regular team and management meetings are an important method of keeping people informed and answering their questions. Treat these meetings seriously. Unarranged meetings are also valuable, with any number of attendees from two upward. They require less formality but should be brief. Keep written notes of what has been decided or what needs to be done, and circulate the notes so that staff feel that they are fully involved.

GAINING TRUST AND COMMITMENT

A committed employee is extraordinarily valuable. You can gain staff commitment by meeting people's key needs, paying attention to people at all levels, trusting and being trusted, tolerating individuality, and creating a blame-free, "can-do" culture.

19 Give staff the opportunity to show that you can trust them.

QUESTIONS TO ASK YOURSELF

Q Do you trust others enough so you can delegate effectively?

Q Will you leave the delegate, after briefing, to complete the job without interference?

Q Do you show people that you trust them not to let you down?

Q Do you rely on rules and regulations to judge other people's work?

Q Do you instill trust in others by always being truthful and keeping your promises?

NURTURING TRUST

The quality and style of leadership are major factors in gaining employees' trust and commitment. Clear decision-making should be coupled with a collaborative, collegiate approach. This entails taking people into your confidence and explicitly and openly valuing their contributions. You should also make yourself as visible as possible, and show yourself to be approachable and willing to listen to others. People respond well to a collective ambition with which they can identify. Remember that to earn trust, you must first learn to trust those who work for you.

◄ WINNING TRUST
These are the key managerial qualities that inspire trust and commitment in employees. Work on developing such qualities in yourself to help create a fully committed workforce.

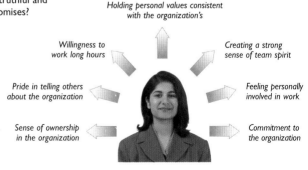

Holding personal values consistent with the organization's

Willingness to work long hours

Creating a strong sense of team spirit

Pride in telling others about the organization

Feeling personally involved in work

Sense of ownership in the organization

Commitment to the organization

WINNING MINDS, SPIRITS, AND HEARTS

The full commitment of staff cannot be realized unless you address people's psychological needs. Research has shown that most management activities are directed toward intellectual needs, some attention is paid to the expression of individuality, but even less attention is paid to emotional needs. By giving equal weight to all three areas, you are more likely to win the minds, spirits, and hearts of your employees. The means to achieve this include: allowing people some autonomy in creating their work environment; making them feel valued by openly recognizing their achievements; and empowering them by handing over as much control as possible in their areas of responsibility.

20 Make sure you address people's intellectual and emotional needs.

21 Listen to unhappy employees – they may reveal serious problems.

Remains loyal, despite unvoiced complaints

Loyal and enthusiastic

CHAMPION

WALKING WOUNDED

Highly critical of the company

Disenchanted and unproductive

DETRACTOR

MISSING IN ACTION

◀ **DEGREES OF COMMITMENT**
You must understand your staff in order to develop true commitment. One marketing classification of four customer types also applies to employees. Aim to build communication policies that reach those "missing in action," and identify the "walking wounded" and the "detractors." Then devise programs that will take them into the "champion" ranks.

22 Endeavor to transform all employees into "champions."

KEEPING STAFF COMMITTED

One of the most effective ways of keeping employees committed and raising retention, is to enrich their jobs and increase motivation. This can be achieved by a number of means, including raising interest levels, ensuring that each employee has a stimulating variety of tasks to perform, and providing the resources and training through which new skills can be developed. A multiskilled employee will be able to perform a range of interesting tasks, while a person with limited skills may be prone to boredom through repetition. Continually encouraging your staff to make suggestions for efficiency improvements will further motivate them, as well as give them a sense of involvement in a task or project and commitment to its success.

23 Investigate fully whenever figures for employee retention start to drop significantly.

▼ **DIFFERING PERCEPTIONS**
A survey conducted in several different organizations revealed that managers, in contrast to employees, have greater confidence in the personal development factors their organization provides.

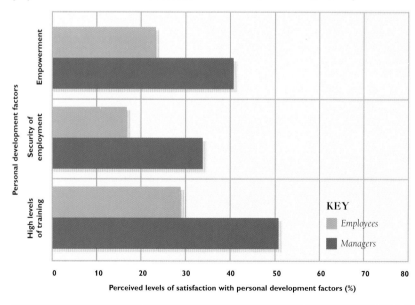

KEY

Employees

Managers

Personal development factors

Empowerment

Security of employment

High levels of training

0   10   20   30   40   50   60   70   80

Perceived levels of satisfaction with personal development factors (%)

REWARDING EXCELLENCE

Acknowledging excellence is vital in maintaining an employee's commitment and job satisfaction. Consider rewarding exceptional performance and high productivity with financial incentives. These could include one-time salary raises, bonus payments, or, if appropriate, stock options. If an employee has substantially reduced the company's costs, this could also be financially rewarded. For more modest levels of achievement, other benefits – such as inclusion on senior staff training weekends – are highly motivating. Above all, never underestimate the value of a simple "thank you."

QUESTIONS TO ASK YOURSELF

Q Have I devised financial reward programs for excellence?

Q Have I considered non-monetary rewards?

Q Do I always say "thank you" when a job is done well?

Q Am I creating "heroes" that other staff can admire?

24 Ensure you involve everybody in a personal project.

PROJECT ▶ "HERO"
Recognition of a popular leader encourages others to show commitment.

Success is publicly celebrated

Employee's self-belief is bolstered

STAYING POSITIVE

To create a positive environment within your organization, it is important to create a "can-do" atmosphere. This should be built on mutual trust, in which people, whatever their self-doubts, are sure that the organization can achieve whatever it is asked to do. Actual achievement is essential to foster this confidence. Start group projects at every opportunity, choosing tasks that have a clear purpose and a positive, measurable outcome. Also, seek to create "heroes" – well-respected and productive employees (including project leaders) that other staff members admire. Be sure to celebrate each hero's successes: this not only bolsters the hero's self-belief, but also encourages others to trust in the can-do culture and to commit to the organization's goals.

ADJUSTING YOUR APPROACH

How you manage people has a deep impact on their behavior. It is useful to alter and direct your management methods to suit different people and different situations. Your aim is always to encourage people to motivate and manage themselves.

25 Apply discipline, but combine it with empowerment and trust.

COMBINING MANAGEMENT STYLES

Use Theory X to provide foundation of discipline → *Staff carry out instructions*

Use Theory Y to exploit employees' natural desire to succeed → *Employees act on own initiative*

Mix Theory X and Y to motivate, inspire, and continually challenge the team → *Peak performance is achieved*

26 People who enjoy their work will produce the best results.

THEORY X MANAGEMENT

The traditional "order and obey" approach to managing people can be an effective way of motivating them. Tell staff what to do and how to do it, and they either perform as ordered or pay the penalty, with dismissal as the last resort (sometimes the first). Researcher Douglas McGregor named this style Theory X management. You need a bedrock of Theory X discipline in any organization.

THEORY Y MANAGEMENT

In contrast to the Theory X approach, Theory Y states that self-discipline springs from enjoying responsibility. The better educated and skilled your workforce, the more you can rely on these natural drives. Theory Y works well only when people have strong objectives. Combine Theory X and Y to achieve the most effective management.

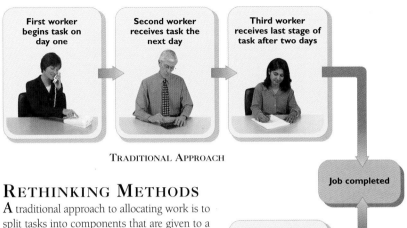

TRADITIONAL APPROACH

RETHINKING METHODS

A traditional approach to allocating work is to split tasks into components that are given to a number of different workers. Although this gives you a high degree of control, it can be monotonous for staff. Also, because the task "waits" in a new line at every desk, this method tends to be inefficient. A better idea is to entrust all or most of a task to one person. This is quicker and more motivating, as the individual feels "ownership" of the task, even though that means more responsibility.

Job completed

MULTI-TASKING

▲ **OWNING THE PROJECT**
Allocating a task to a single employee not only reduces the time needed to complete it, but also promotes job satisfaction.

27 Most people prefer responsibility over too little work.

28 Cut down layers after reforming processes.

CONSULTING PEOPLE

Aim to be flexible in your approach to people, but avoid following one system one day and another the next. Regularly ask your staff what they would like from you. They may like more responsibility or, conversely, more guidance – try to comply with their wishes as far as you can, while serving the best interests of the team.

DEVELOPING PEOPLE

Helping individuals to achieve their potential is in the best interests of the person and the organization. Aim to train, encourage, and provide opportunities for willing people.

PROVIDING TRAINING

Developing the abilities of staff at all levels is so important that some organizations have their own education facilities, and many engage outside trainers and advisers. Top-quality training and development are vital to all organizations.

> **29** Make training the last thing you cut back, never the first.

> **30** Ask people about their long-term goals and aspirations, and assist in their realization.

ARRANGING TRAINING

Try to allocate a percentage of revenues to training (1.5 percent at least), or to lay down minimum training hours – five days per year is a reasonable target. If such policies are sacrificed under short-term financial pressure, your organization loses the benefit of better-trained employees, and it is implied that training is not essential. Provide training that is *specific*, to improve current performance; *general*, to provide wider skills; and *in advance*, to prepare for promotion and change.

EVALUATING FORMS OF STAFF DEVELOPMENT

TYPE OF TRAINING	BENEFITS AND REINFORCEMENTS
TECHNICAL Training in the specifics of a particular job – usually provided in-house and during working hours by specialist instructors or supervisors.	● Enables high-quality performance of tasks. ● Must be repeated at regular intervals to maintain newly enhanced skills. ● Best coupled with an exam that gives a qualification.
QUALITY Training in the principles of total quality, together with the technical tools required for improvement – needs specialist instruction.	● Provides both "quick fixes" for immediate problems and longer-term, organization-wide benefits. ● Instils a philosophy of continuous practical improvement. ● Must be sustained indefinitely to become a way of life.
SKILLS Financial accounting, creative thinking, speaking, IT, writing, presentation, chairing, languages, interviewing, selling, etc. – in-house or external.	● All employees benefit from a general, multi-skill grounding. ● Nervousness about using skills in public is cured. ● Opportunities for practice are needed to build and maintain effectiveness.
PROFESSIONAL Education to obtain qualifications, for example, in accounting, law, banking, engineering – external and either full-time or part-time.	● Provides portable skills, which are valuable to the individual as well as to the employer. ● Specialization leads to a more select choice of future appointments in the organization. ● Requires effort over a considerable period.
FUNCTIONAL Education in marketing, planning, sales management, purchasing, human resources management, etc. – external, but not usually full-time.	● Functional training almost always leads to better performance and improved career paths. ● Must be linked with appointment to functional role. ● Area is often wrongly ignored by companies who simply "hope for the best."
ACTIVITY "Outward Bound"-type courses, in which people learn leadership and teamwork by engaging in physical tasks, such as rock climbing.	● Provides an effective means of team bonding and re-energizing the workforce. ● Must be supplemented by and coordinated with more direct management training.
MANAGERIAL Providing expertise and knowledge in fields such as strategy and change management – business school focus, either internal or external.	● Managers identify, work on, and solve real corporate problems. ● Invaluable grounding if learning is applied to the job. ● Both sides benefit if student remains committed.

IMPROVING SKILLS

Aim to train your staff in as many specific skills as possible. Mental abilities matter greatly in modern organizations, as do the skills needed to master computers. Training in thought processes will improve the execution of practical tasks.

31 Teach people to think analytically – this will benefit the whole organization.

THINKING CLEARLY

Like any other skill, thinking can be taught and improved on. The ability to analyze is basic to this, revolving around the question "Why?" – "Why do we need to cut our price?" or "Why have profits fallen?". Encourage your staff to analyze their work and to ask questions constantly. Analysis requires a high degree of mental organization, which can improve with practice if analysis is part of the corporate way of life.

USING MULTI-SKILLING

The more skills in which a person is trained, the more valuable they are as an employee and the greater their personal potential. In "manufacturing cells" within some factories, employees are given responsibility for an entire product – from initial research to sourcing materials, manufacture, and marketing. The people are interchangeable, which makes them flexible and provides them with a useful knowledge of each other's work. Office work can follow the same ideas on a project basis. Widening people's skills cuts down on cost and time, provides greater flexibility, and greatly encourages team spirit and collaboration.

WORKING IN "CELLS" ▼
Provide people with opportunities to operate in working cells or groups. They will learn the skills of other members of the group, which will increase their effectiveness and improve morale.

32 Get staff into the habit of constantly improving their range of skills.

▼ USING NEW TECHNOLOGY

Make sure that everybody who possibly can be is computer-literate. Both the individual and the organization will suffer in the long term if new technology is not mastered.

> **33** Invest heavily in training for key computer skills: this will improve the performance of your company.

On-line course gives practical experience

A trained employee benefits the company

Study aids help develop new skills

MASTERING COMPUTERS

The use of electronics in business is growing so fast that you should regard technology such as computers as something that everybody must know how to use. If your organization does not have an Intranet (internal computer system) or some way of connecting people and files, you must press hard for the installation of such a set-up. If portable computers can improve operations (for instance, those of service engineers), try to provide them. There will be problems to resolve, ranging from security and privacy to the overuse of email. But all these obstacles can be overcome. More difficulties will be created unless everybody who can usefully become computer-literate is given the necessary training and equipment.

QUESTIONS TO ASK YOURSELF

Q Have my staff been sufficiently trained in computer skills?

Q Is their training both up-to-date and updated regularly?

Q Do people have opportunities to practice their new skills in order to master them?

Q Have I listened to other people's suggestions regarding new technology?

Q Does the organization have sufficient technical support?

Q Is the company using all the computer programs available to improve performance?

GUIDING OTHERS

All managers coach. They tell people what they are doing right or wrong on the job, train them, assess them, and counsel them. The mentor's role overlaps with those of the coach and the counselor, but the three roles have separate purposes.

34 If mistakes are made, ask yourself if you played any part in them.

BEING A COACH

Giving clear instructions about what you expect is the first step of coaching. This stage often produces a drop in motivation as reality challenges the employee's ability. At this point you become a helper, coaching the employee to recognize his or her strengths and to form ambitions. Finally, the person is in control of him- or herself and the job. You then step aside and assume the role of adviser, to be consulted when needed.

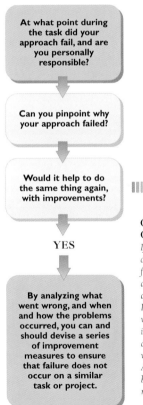

At what point during the task did your approach fail, and are you personally responsible?

Can you pinpoint why your approach failed?

Would it help to do the same thing again, with improvements?

YES

By analyzing what went wrong, and when and how the problems occurred, you can and should devise a series of improvement measures to ensure that failure does not occur on a similar task or project.

NO

COACHING QUESTIONS
If someone you are coaching has experienced failure in his or her work, ask the person these questions in sequence. It may be that his or her work efforts can be improved with simple adjustments to current working methods. Alternatively, the person's basic approach to tasks may need reassessing.

Did you plan the task and, if so, how?

What wrong decisions were made?

What must you do differently next time?

Design a program to correct defects.

▼ GUIDING OBJECTIVELY
Use your years of work experience and your knowledge of the organization to steer junior employees along the most appropriate career paths.

Experienced manager coaches an employee, helping his development

BEING A MENTOR

A mentor is a senior manager who establishes a special relationship with a particular junior. As a mentor, you should never be in a line relationship with the mentored (a "line" being the route along which orders pass from the top of the organization to the bottom), otherwise you cannot guarantee a disinterested, objective viewpoint. Do not consider mentoring only in times of trouble. Instead, take a continuous interest in the progress of the junior. He or she will expect to discuss work difficulties with you, and you can intervene with line managers if the situation demands it.

Employee receives valuable guidance and encouragement

BEING A COUNSELOR

As a counselor you are called upon to deal with personal problems. These may be problems at work or home. Either way, the junior employee needs to tell a sympathetic listener about his or her troubles. You should ideally help the person to find his or her own solution, though it may be necessary to make strong suggestions. Usually, the employee will turn to an immediate superior, especially since the problem may demand time off. Never turn away from a counseling need, and call in others (possibly outside experts) if the problem is beyond your powers.

35 Find every junior a wise mentor who gives good advice.

36 Encourage employees to suggest ways to solve problems.

TEACHING BY EXAMPLE

As the boss of a group you are likely to be a prime role model – the person who sets the tone of the unit. You must also create the right atmosphere for successful teamwork and use example purposefully to teach and encourage good practice.

37 Use opportunities to lead from the front and set a good example.

38 Teach by showing how, not by giving people your orders.

ACTING AS A ROLE MODEL

Employees expect their manager to set a positive example. It is therefore very important that you neither fall below the high standards that you set yourself nor behave disparagingly to members of staff who do fall short of them. Above all, you should behave consistently at all times.

COMPETENCE

SUPPORTIVENESS

CHARISMA

FAIR-MINDEDNESS

HONESTY

INSPIRING PEOPLE
According to research, there are ten personal qualities that are the most admired characteristics of respected organizational leaders. These qualities are less to do with making the right or wrong decisions and more to do with integrity and straightforward behavior.

VISION

INTELLIGENCE

COURAGE

BROAD-MINDEDNESS

DIRECTNESS

SHARING SKILLS

Team members often make very effective teachers, either by tutoring less experienced members or by sharing different sets of skills. You should consider an organized, on-the-job program of development with one team member sitting by another to learn about their job. This will help both parties reach a deeper understanding of the work of the team, as well as transferring new skills. You can achieve a similar effect by forming a mini-team or task force to tackle a particular issue, not necessarily related to the team's main objective. Adopting a strategy like this ensures that team members learn how to develop solutions and turn them into action.

CULTURAL DIFFERENCES

The emphasis placed on teaching varies from country to country, but the Japanese in particular place great importance on action learning. Germans tend to be more formal, expecting people to follow instructions. Americans are more likely to have been taught about managing and will often adopt new "empowering" methods, which may later be neglected. English managers are likely to improvise and regard skills as natural, untaught assets.

39 Bring in outside trainers as often as possible.

Colleague is able to learn by practicing skills

◀ **LEARNING ON THE JOB**
Action learning is more effective than sedentary learning involving books and lectures. Encourage more experienced staff members to take the lead.

Senior employee explains job to colleague

NURTURING TALENT

Identifying and using individual talent is one of the most satisfying and productive aspects of a manager's work. Finding good people is only part of the task – talented people can be difficult to manage, but the effort is well worthwhile.

40 Regard staff losses as opportunities to introduce new strengths.

QUESTIONS TO ASK ABOUT OTHERS

Q Do they have, or could they develop, a special expertise?

Q Can they combine talents such as research and management?

Q Do they show signs of organizational ability?

Q Are they successful at bringing in new business?

Q Have they shown the ability to lead others?

FINDING TALENT

Individual talents within organizations, especially large ones, are often underemployed or even unnoticed. Look out for signs of abilities that are not being fully used (or used at all) and find ways in which the individuals concerned can contribute more. People who engage in non-work activities, like running a company social club or event, may be sources of untapped talent. Bringing talent to the foreground not only relaunches the individual's career, but also strengthens the organization's success potential.

PLANNING SUCCESSION

The more successful subordinates are, the more likely they are to leave your company for "better" things. You should welcome this, as you are the friend and supporter who has helped them to develop and display their talents. However, their promotion will leave gaps. You should always have an answer to the question "What will I do if Jean or John leaves?". This may create an opportunity to reorganize work so that a replacement is not needed. More likely, you will be able to reward someone with promotion, thereby creating another vacancy. Maintain a succession folder, regularly update it, and pencil in potential successors for every key job.

41 Promote talented individuals, even if they excel in their current job.

42 Speak out if you believe someone is being moved to the wrong job.

| Personal qualities of drive and perseverance | Ability to form relationships and to communicate | | Ability to identify and to recognize individual talent | Target-setting, appraising, coaching, and giving feedback |

THE INDIVIDUAL'S CONTRIBUTION

THE ORGANIZATION'S CONTRIBUTION

| Energy and strong needs, drives, and motives | Continual willingness to learn and develop | | Giving rewards, incentives, and recognition | Investment in personnel training and development |

DEVELOPING ▲ TALENT
The development of talent depends equally on input from both the organization and the individual.

MAXIMUM DEVELOPMENT OF INDIVIDUAL TALENT

FOCUSING ON CONTRIBUTION

What is your attitude toward people who are "difficult, demanding, disagreeable, disobedient, dislikable, disorganized, disputing, disrespectful, and discordant"? An obvious answer is that you do not want them around. But the "9D" characteristics, according to American consultant Michael J. Kami, are those of the "talented gorillas," who may be the most productive employees you have. Above all, concentrate on people's contributions, not their personalities.

UNCONVENTIONAL EMPLOYEE ▶
Nonconformist staff members may be difficult to manage, but are sometimes the most productive.

Unorthodox appearance may accompany willingness and talent

ENCOURAGING MANAGEMENT POTENTIAL

Avoid typecasting people and being typecast. Your staff may have abilities that go well beyond their present roles, and that will take them upward in the organization – perhaps into management.

43 Seek to promote from within in the first instance.

44 Encourage staff to apply for any internal openings.

POINTS TO REMEMBER

● People's abilities are more likely to be underestimated than rated too highly.

● Classroom learning is an essential element of management development.

● Lack of ability can usually be improved with training.

SPOTTING ABILITIES

The fact that somebody has mastered a particular job gives grounds for supposing that he or she could advance to higher levels. When vacancies or opportunities occur, always look first to see whether someone already employed in the organization could fill the post. Remember that technical deficiencies can generally be overcome by training. Look for personal characteristics (such as energy and perseverance), good interpersonal behavior, strong motivation, the ability and willingness to learn, excellent organizational skills, and flexibility. Task forces and other ad hoc groups provide a relatively risk-free way of testing whether a person has the ability to rise.

RECOGNIZING ▶ MANAGEMENT QUALITIES
More people have management ability than is commonly supposed. Look out for employees with these key qualities, and earmark them for future promotion to management posts.

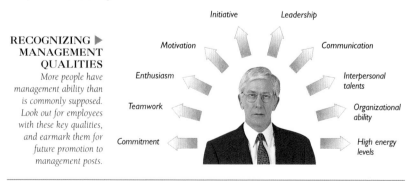

Initiative

Leadership

Motivation

Communication

Enthusiasm

Interpersonal talents

Teamwork

Organizational ability

Commitment

High energy levels

MAKING MANAGERS

In your search for management potential, remember that management is not a rarefied activity requiring a high degree of education. Although managers are supposed to spend their time on intellectual activities – such as planning, organizing, and coordinating – in reality their days are very fragmented and dominated by practical matters. They may have only half an hour of uninterrupted work every two days. You need to ask yourself if the person you are considering for promotion is capable of working effectively in these conditions. If your potential manager prefers to work on only one task at a time, then elevation to management may not be appropriate.

45 Allow people to show that they can manage.

▼ **COPING WITH PRESSURE**
Aspiring managers should be practical and able to handle several tasks at once. Give people the chance to demonstrate their ability and they may well prove to be candidates for promotion.

Employee is able to cope with interruptions

Several duties are managed simultaneously

46 Train staff for higher duties as early as you can.

47 Make a list of good coworkers and keep it for future reference.

FACILITATING PROMOTION

You may be tempted to keep people where they are – doing a good job – rather than move them onward and upward. Not promoting people is bad for their career development and for the organization, which is not using talent to the full. Some organizations even refuse to train adequately because they are frightened of losing the trained employee to someone else: this condemns them to having an undertrained labor force. Reconcile yourself to the fact that people are likely to move on from time to time. If you think the move is good for them, encourage and congratulate them.

MOTIVATING PEOPLE

Receiving orders is far less motivating than taking part in planning and decision-making. Enable your staff to achieve their ambitions and to manage themselves in order to achieve the desired results.

48 Use the strategic thinking of all employees.

MOTIVATING FACTORS

FACTOR	ACTION
SELF-FULFILLMENT	Enable employees to take on challenges.
RECOGNITION	Tell employees how well they are doing.
PEER RESPECT	Celebrate the individual's success publicly.
EXPERTISE	Encourage development of special knowledge.
COMPETENCE	Provide training to develop key skills.
ACHIEVEMENT	Agree on targets that are achievable.
AUTONOMY	Allow employees to plan and design own work.
SELF-CONFIDENCE	Make sure that allocated tasks can be done well.
SELF-RESPECT	Increase the individual's regard for self.
MEMBERSHIP	Ensure employees enter "club" of coworkers.

SHARING THE STRATEGY

It is very important to inform people about strategic plans and their own part in achieving the strategies. Take trouble to improve their understanding and to win their approval, as this will have a highly positive influence on performance. Never forget that employees invest their lives and financial security in the company.

Manager explains how task relates to overall strategy

▲ **ENRICHING A JOB**
Give people jobs that enable them to feel good about the organization and its management.

DELEGATING DECISIONS

> **49** Allow others to make decisions that they can make just as well as you.

Pushing the power of decision-making downward reduces pressure on senior management. It also motivates people on the lower levels because it gives them a vote of confidence. And, because the decision is taken nearer to the point of action, it is more likely to be correct. The main reasons for hoarding decisions that could be taken lower down are bad ones: you want to keep the decision power all to yourself, or you do not trust those in positions below to get things right (which calls into question the appropriateness of your appointments). You should certainly take all the decisions that only you as a manager can make; but even then you can draw on all the valuable input available from colleagues and subordinates.

HANDING DOWN POWER

MANAGEMENT DECISIONS
The manager sets out the agenda for a particular task, decides on the powers she must keep for herself, and selects the people who she thinks will best carry out the delegated duties.

DELEGATED DECISIONS
The delegates each have a clearly defined role that they have helped establish. They choose their own working methods, make decisions as necessary, and are responsible for meeting the agreed aim.

INTRODUCING SELF-MANAGEMENT

The standard approach to establishing self-management among staff is to define individual job requirements so that employees can carry out the processes effectively. This is contradictory because somebody other than the self-manager is managing the tasks, and probably explaining how to do the tasks as well. Motivational empowerment only develops if you can answer "yes" to four key questions (right). If any answers are "no," reassess your approach to self-management.

QUESTIONS TO ASK YOURSELF

Q Do individuals define their own tasks?

Q Do they define the behavior that is required to perform their tasks?

Q Do managers and the managed jointly define performance goals that are challenging for the individual?

Q Do individuals define the importance of the goal?

IMPROVING PERFORMANCE

All improvement programs run out of steam unless you make conscious efforts to renew people's support. Improvement stems from repetition, but greater gains come from focused planning and training.

50 Aim to improve the quality of all company processes.

MANAGING QUALITY

Total Quality Management (TQM) is built around the idea that individuals can always improve their work by learning new techniques and applying them. In TQM workshops people master techniques, such as how to use the "six management and planning tools" required to resolve issues. This may sound complicated, but using such tools speeds up processes, eliminates task stages, and reduces costs quickly. The objective is to cut out waste and to increase customer satisfaction by improving product or service quality, employee performance, and economic value. This approach satisfies people's natural urge to do a better job and to see improvements.

Describe what is going wrong

Collect and analyze facts on the issue

Plan and implement a solution

Confirm that the solution really works

Incorporate the solution into the refined process

Reexamine the process and find any weaknesses

◀ **SIX STEPS TO BETTER QUALITY**
These six steps can be applied by individuals or teams. Encourage staff at all levels to use them to examine and improve processes and systems.

51 Focus quality work on producing real customer benefits.

52 Use training in quality skills to increase people's general ability.

LEARNING BY EXPERIENCE

As people gain experience in a job, they see ways of doing it better, cutting costs, and saving time. Encourage staff to come forward with such ideas – this will improve performance and raise morale. Consider holding regular ideas meetings where people can make constructive suggestions. Such meetings often provide the inspiration for others to develop the ideas further. Always act on these proposals where possible – it is especially motivating if the person who brought forward the original idea is the one to implement it.

53 Listen to staff and ask for their improvement ideas.

54 Expect people to continue achieving better results.

◀ **LEARNING CURVE**
As people gain experience of their work, their performance will naturally improve. The pattern of a learning curve shows how a period of intensive development is followed by a "levelling-off" stage.

Skills learned

Time period

55 Concentrate on one initiative at a time to avoid confusion.

MAINTAINING MOMENTUM

A common mistake is to abandon an improvement initiative before it has a real chance to pay off, and to replace it with another, which then suffers the same fate. This "flavor of the month" policy breeds cynicism and lethargy. A far better policy is to stick to one basic program (such as TQM), but to revise and improve it all the time. At the same time, select new themes for the initiative (say, every year) to refocus and renew the forward drive. In a large team or department you could involve different groups in developing the new themes, and in this way everyone will feel more committed to the programme. The focus one year could be on responding to customers, the next target could be streamlining in-house systems, and the next could be boosting quality – but all of them would be aiming to deliver what the customer wants more quickly and cost-effectively.

MAKING PROGRESS

The more responsibility you give to people, the greater their interest and productivity are likely to be. The same principle applies to their knowledge of the organization and how they contribute to its success – the more knowledge, the better.

56 Make "right the first time" a key aim for everybody in your team.

QUESTIONS TO ASK YOURSELF

Q Do I enable people to take pride in the quality of their own work?

Q Do I constantly look for ways to increase group morale?

Q Have I considered setting up specialist groups within my organization?

Q Am I making best use of a deployment policy and annual review?

Q Am I setting objectives that will motivate people?

GETTING IT RIGHT THE FIRST TIME

Make people responsible for the quality of their own work and it will usually inspire them to do better. Quality used to be maintained by trained inspectors who would check the work and send back anything imperfect – an expensive and wasteful method. Instead, increase training and assistance to help people produce only perfect work in the first place. Use supervisors as "enablers" who help groups and individuals whenever needed. This will keep work that needs redoing to a minimum, and should allow you to greatly reduce the numbers of supervisors.

RAISING GROUP MORALE

High group morale can enrich individual motivation and performance remarkably. In difficult situations, when companies are in crisis and can only be saved by major effort, group morale often rises to far higher levels than before. Individual objections and objectives are bypassed in the collective drive to do what must be done. But you need not wait until crisis strikes to instil this attitude in your staff. This does not mean you have to create an artificial emergency: build urgency by setting important objectives to which everyone subscribes and has a clear, agreed plan for reaching.

57 Expect people to supervise their own performance.

58 Encourage acceptance of and desire for change at all times.

USING POLICY DEPLOYMENT

Policy deployment may sound daunting, but it is based on simple principles. First, a vision of the company's future is developed with the help of all its staff. "Improvement themes" are selected, again with people's help, that will produce better results. The themes, such as "Getting it Right the First Time" or "Increasing Competitive Advantage," generate objectives for every unit and everyone in every unit. Detailed plans are made for the theme's implementation, and progress is reviewed every month. An annual review is also necessary to modify the vision and associated themes when necessary. The goal is to align individual and team ambitions with those of the organization. Everyone, from the chief executive downwards, shares in the vision and the strategy for realizing it, and knows their own part in achieving it.

**ENRICHING JOBS ▶
USING DEPLOYMENT**
By involving everyone in the organization with a new corporate vision and plans to realize that vision, you can enrich jobs and greatly increase people's motivation levels.

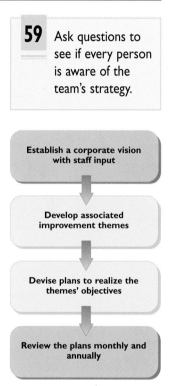

59 Ask questions to see if every person is aware of the team's strategy.

Establish a corporate vision with staff input

Develop associated improvement themes

Devise plans to realize the themes' objectives

Review the plans monthly and annually

OUTSOURCING TO INCREASE PROFITABILITY

Many companies have "outsourced" jobs by establishing their employees as independent suppliers of products or services. Sometimes these moves are driven by negative cost-cutting motives, which often backfire. Used positively, the approach enables the company to retain the services of highly skilled experts, whose full-time employment is not justified (for example). In return, the employees gain the freedom to work profitably on their own terms. The flexibility that outsourcing offers can enrich people's working lives greatly. You can, however, enrich jobs in this way without cutting the employee loose from the organization by creating a "firm within the firm" – an expert, in-house group with specific responsibilities.

FINDING SOLUTIONS

Sensitive interpersonal skills are essential for creating a comfortable and productive working environment. Use your skills to resolve individual difficulties and to deal with conflicts.

BUILDING ENVIRONMENTS

Creating an atmosphere in which people feel appreciated and an essential part of a team is a challenge for every manager. A successful effort in this direction, however, will reduce the likelihood of problems.

60 If a group grows too large, divide it into smaller parts.

▲ **TEAM SPIRIT**
Encourage the workforce to consider themselves as an elite, closely knit team. A good analogy is a united football team.

ENSURING COHESION

An employee who feels neglected and who is excluded from a cohesive working group is more likely to be unmotivated and prone to dissatisfaction than the person who has support and recognition from colleagues and managers. Encourage people to react positively and make effective contributions. This can be done by creating structures in which each staff member identifies with a group in which the responsibilities are clearly understood by all. An unselfish interest in the success of other group members is generated in a team that is closely bound together by common goals.

CONTROLLING OFFICE POLITICS

Strong feelings are aroused by the subject of office politics – anyone who has worked in an office will have experienced its effects. The negative side of office politics surfaces when it is used by individuals to increase personal power at the expense of colleagues and/or the organization. Strive to create a working environment in which status and hierarchy have as little importance as possible and the politics will stop.

61 Celebrate the achievements of your organization.

62 Whenever you can, involve people in specific tasks with clear aims.

CASE STUDY

Jan, a shopfloor worker, noticed that every so often her department had to write off stocks of components that had become obsolete. This was obviously expensive, and she wondered why the stock control was so ineffective. She found that the excess was held as "buffer stock" in case supplies became short. She reasoned that the cost of holding the stock must be so high that putting in a better system for ordering and locating needed parts would pay for itself many times over. Jan received full support from management and her colleagues to begin an improvement project, which she led from start to finish. She enlisted the help of other colleagues in completing her project. The stocks held in the department were halved, and the obsolete and obsolescent items reduced by 90 percent.

◀ ENCOURAGING INITIATIVE

Jan was encouraged by her superiors to embark on what could be termed a one-person "Quality Improvement Project" (QIP). Such projects involve detailed studies of significant areas where money is being wasted. They are only possible in working environments that support and nurture the initiative of the individual.

USING POSITIVE EMOTIONS

An openness and responsiveness to people's spontaneity and originality will generate a positive atmosphere in which creative ideas can flourish and demotivating boredom is reduced. Informality, and a reasonably tolerant acceptance of your staff's inevitable mistakes, will also generate an environment in which recognition for success, rather than blame for failure, is the dominant culture. Take every opportunity to generate excitement over what the company and individuals have achieved and what challenges must be met for the future of the organization.

OPENING CLOSED MINDS

People are often reluctant to accept ideas from outside sources. The "Not Invented Here" (NIH) syndrome occurs when individuals ignore ideas from other parts of the organization or other companies. Discourage this syndrome among your staff.

63 Clearly emphasize that new ideas will not be rejected as a matter of course.

ACCEPTING IDEAS

The consequences of NIH are often expensive and sometimes disastrous. Antidotes must come from the organization's management. Welcome all ideas, accept those that are good, and explain the reasons for any rejections. This will ensure a flow of ideas, and people will be encouraged to see plans as opportunities, rather than threats, and to welcome them. Also, encourage people to act as "spies," reporting on any good ideas they have spotted in other organizations, businesses, or countries.

Manager listens to idea and suggests changes

Employee's confidence is boosted

WELCOMING INPUT ▲
Always give new ideas careful thought and consideration. If you dismiss them, the flow of ideas will soon start to dry up.

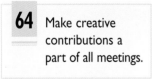

64 Make creative contributions a part of all meetings.

ENCOURAGING CREATIVITY

Creativity involves exploring and adopting new ideas that may produce better results. Many people believe that they are uncreative: in fact, everybody has potential and can be taught resourceful techniques. Stage workshops in which people can apply their skills to real-life issues. People are often reluctant because they fear that the new approach may fail. Explain that not taking risks can lead to rivals seizing the best opportunities.

CHANGING MIND-SETS

Remember that people have a logical basis for rejecting a creative plan. Saying "no" means that no further action need be taken; saying "yes" may well mean extra work, as well as extra risk. People who start new projects and fail often suffer as a result, whereas managers are seldom sacked for the opportunities they missed. This helps to develop negative mind-sets, which mean that people spot the reasons for doing nothing and miss the benefits from taking new action. You can change negative mind-sets into positive ones by starting special projects that require creativity and by providing incentives for those involved. Regularly monitor such new initiatives, and ensure that senior management are aware of any progress or success and of who has contributed effectively.

Establish a
special creative project to
encourage initiative

Include non-managerial
staff who will work effectively
in a team

Insist that such
new initiatives are recognized
throughout the company

Openly celebrate the
positive results of the creative
projects

CREATING POSITIVE MIND-SETS ▶
Provide incentives for creativity. Encourage managers to include in their monthly reports any creative initiatives that were taken in the period, who was involved, and what is planned for the future.

65 Always insist that opportunities are seized after the risks are assessed.

66 Stress that not taking risks is usually due to lack of self-confidence.

TAKING RISKS

Since you want people to be active and to show initiative, you must make it clear that risk-taking is encouraged. Otherwise, the normal human tendency to prefer the known to the unknown will inhibit progress both inside the company and in the marketplace. Risk can be defined as "incurring the chance of unfortunate consequences by doing something." You should not let the threat of unfortunate consequences prevent action. Reward successful risk-taking, and do not penalize failure except in two circumstances:
- The person has not carefully analyzed and understood the risks before acting;
- The person has repeated past mistakes.

DEALING WITH CONFLICT

Conflict is unavoidable when people interact at work. If faced with conflict or an angry person, adopt a positive and rational approach to defuse any heightened emotions, then look for a resolution based on pragmatism and compromise.

67 Remember that you are concerned with behavior, not with character.

QUESTIONS TO ASK YOURSELF

Q Where is the problem and what is it exactly?

Q What are the potential solutions?

Q Which solution out of all the alternatives is the best?

Q How is the solution best implemented?

FACING PROBLEMS

Dealing with conflicts between employees is an inevitable part of managerial life. Once you are aware of conflict, take immediate action and invite the disagreeing parties to voice their points of view in a meeting. The key is to minimize the emotive element and to substitute it with a rational pragmatism. Even if you believe one position to be correct, be prepared to consider the other point of view; if it is valid, then try to reach a compromise.

▼ **FINDING A SOLUTION**
Provide an environment where disagreeing employees can openly voice their problems and then work toward effecting a resolution.

Employee freely airs his point of view

Manager acts as arbiter

Plans for a solution to the conflict are noted

Employee voices her opinion

DEFUSING NEGATIVE EMOTIONS

Guilt, anxiety, and anger are common negative emotions that must be managed carefully. Try to impress upon your employees that guilt will not repair whatever action has caused the upset, that anxiety will not prevent a future event that causes fear, and that anger is not an appropriate or helpful response to any situation. A person usually reacts angrily because others have not acted as he or she wants. You can defuse this anger by presenting a more reasonable point of view.

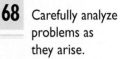

68 Carefully analyze problems as they arise.

69 Ask a close colleague to help defuse your anger.

DEALING WITH ANGER

Discussing the negative effects of anger with a disgruntled employee may help to resolve a situation of conflict. Beset by emotions that will probably have been growing in intensity over a period of time, the person will benefit from your rational observations of their inappropriate and misdirected behavior and your suggestions for dealing with these feelings.

SIGNS OF ANGER

- Projecting bad feelings onto others, and resorting to sarcasm and ridicule.
- Avoiding the need for rational, unemotional responses.
- Concealing the loss of an argument, and making excuses for failure.
- Making excuses for intimidating and manipulating others.

ANTIDOTES TO OFFER

- Analyze the reasons behind angry feelings.
- Remember that it is possible to disapprove without being angry.
- Turn to a trusted, uninvolved friend before venting your anger.
- Ask whether expectations of others are reasonable.
- Expect to be disagreed with and displeased sometimes.
- Apologize to the objects of anger.

◀ **REGAINING COMPOSURE**
By addressing some of the reasons and emotions behind a person's anger, you may be able to help them regain their composure.

WORKING COLLECTIVELY

If general conflicts arise, resolutions may be found through a frank and open airing of grievances, or by rethinking current working methods. Unions can play a vital part in the proceedings as intermediaries between an organization and its employees.

70 Encourage your workers to recognize your management skills.

71 Avoid demonizing a union or any one person, but treat issues on merit.

▼ **BEING POSITIVE**
When negotiating, restructuring, or resolving disputes, always seek a firm conclusion, and use a working method that strengthens people's natural instincts to be full members of a winning team.

RESOLVING CONFLICT

If conflict occurs within teams, you must work quickly to identify its causes and to implement workable, mutually agreed solutions. Consider whether a disruptive conflict is growing between two or more members that is affecting the rest of the team, or if the group as a whole is expressing general dissatisfaction with an issue. Conflicts between individuals should be resolved through firm but even-handed intervention. You may need to change the membership of the team to resolve the issue finally.

HANDLING UNIONS

Employers tend to regard unions as the enemy, vice versa, but an orderly, sympathetic union can be helpful to a well-run organization. Employees like to have representatives who can look after their interests more effectively than they can as individuals. Do not, however, make the mistake of identifying the union as the workforce: your contract is with each employee. Reserve for the union only those matters that belong to the union (representing individuals in dismissals, for example), and treat union officials with the same respect you would show any associate.

72 Never give in to demands that are unreasonable, but seek compromise.

STANDING FIRM ▶
Alan's new working methods gave the workers much more say in their work, which improved quality and reduced costs. This enabled Alan to raise pay while still making large savings.

CASE STUDY

Alan was appointed to run the maintenance operation for a large vehicle fleet. It depended on skilled, unionized workers who had a long history of trouble-making. A strike broke out shortly after Alan took charge. The workers, testing the new boss, demanded pay raises that the operation could not afford. They would not make any concessions. Alan also stood firm, and the

staff walked out. Calling his managers together, Alan offered a package that addressed some of the employees' grievances. His proposal was eventually accepted, the strike ended, and the staff resumed work. Alan had successfully asserted management's right to manage, but he felt that more needed to be done. He went on to devise new methods of working that would help prevent future conflict.

QUESTIONS TO ASK YOURSELF

Q Is the dispute caused by a deep-seated grievance?

Q How widespread is the dispute?

Q Will a financial reward resolve the problem?

Q Have I taken all factors into consideration?

Q Will the proposed solution be effective in the long term?

CONFRONTING TROUBLE

When major disputes arise, do not stop at analyzing the apparent difficulties. It is essential to look for the underlying causes of the problem. Once the root causes have been identified, you can produce plans for finding effective and long-term tactical solutions – whether they be strategic, financial, or otherwise. If you leave the causes untouched, however, the difficulties will only recur. Your object is not only to cure the present troubles, but to ensure that they are permanently eliminated – with beneficial results for everybody.

DEALING WITH PERSONAL DIFFICULTIES

All managers are ultimately personnel officers. From time to time, you may have to deal with difficult personal matters that your staff bring to you. Take fast action, because such issues rarely improve with time.

73 Encourage people to bring their complaints and problems to you.

Manager asks that grievances be discussed separately.

MEETING NEEDS

Performance at work can be affected by anything from illness and bereavement to marital breakup and financial woes. Whether or not performance suffers, the person concerned requires attention and sympathy. This can take the form of allowing time off, or insisting that it be taken. Often practical assistance is required, perhaps involving money or helping to find legal advice, for example.

◀ **UNEARTHING PROBLEMS**
Aggressive behavior in the workplace may disguise personal difficulties – avoid leaping to conclusions and be prepared to listen.

ENCOURAGING OPENNESS

Develop a personal rapport with your staff – this will help you to recognize any changes in their behavior. If an employee displays unusual irritability, tension, or other negative behavior, do not hesitate to approach them. Do not reprimand them for their work performance, but encourage them to talk openly about their problem. Listen sympathetically. Your availability will contribute to a caring environment in which people feel they can share their concerns.

74 Never take sides in a quarrel – be clearly impartial.

75 Handle personal problems as a friend, not a boss.

CULTURAL DIFFERENCES

British managers tend to be sympathetic to people with difficulties, while Americans and Germans are generally less understanding. The Japanese expect people to work, even in times of personal crisis.

PROVIDING SUPPORT

A manager dealing with a troubled employee must be supportive without getting too involved. Some specific problems – such as alcoholism and other types of compulsive behavior – can require professional help. Display a positive attitude toward therapy and encourage the employee to choose this option. In the workplace, make the employee feel that their services are still needed and valued. This will boost their confidence as well as maintain a level of normality.

Employee explains why her work is suffering

Manager listens and offers advice

◀ **OFFERING SYMPATHY**
It may be that an attentive ear will be enough to meet a need. Sometimes, however, you may have to refer a member of staff to a counselor.

76 Make time to talk to any employee who comes to you with problems.

DEALING WITH GENDER ISSUES

The issue of gender in the workplace goes far beyond harassment, sexual or otherwise. Harassing women is both offensive and an offense and must not be tolerated. There is no acceptable alternative to both practicing and preaching true equality: make sure that all employees are judged by what they contribute to the organization, not by their gender. If one of your employees is being subjected to patronizing behavior, act swiftly. But do not expect to change intolerance overnight. Make the change a key objective, however, and be prepared to take any action necessary to create an atmosphere in which both men and women feel comfortable, and in which any family needs, such as child care, are understood and accommodated.

MANAGING CHANGE

Managers often focus on the mechanics of change, concentrating on ensuring that their plan is followed. If their staff are not satisfied, however, the plan is likely to fail. If you listen to people's needs, they will respond positively to change.

77 Treat resistance to change as a problem that can always be solved.

78 Motivate your staff by acting positively on their creative ideas for change.

79 Use measured, continuous change to stimulate staff and avoid staleness.

BALANCING NEEDS

Some managers fall into the trap of putting production needs ahead of other organizational needs; others put concern for people above that for production. Both styles are erroneous, though the latter is popular with employees. Change, both large and small, is managed effectively only by showing equal concern for both needs. Attention to employees as people, coupled with strong interest in their welfare, well-being, and wishes, pays off in terms of better acceptance of changes and better performance. Change management that pays inadequate attention to people threatens productivity and is likely to misfire.

INVOLVING PEOPLE

When employees feel excluded from the decisions that will determine the way they do their work, demotivation and resentment can be the negative results. Ensure, therefore, that staff are given the opportunity to contribute and involve themselves at many levels of the decision-making process before any changes have to be made. This could range from having a say in how the office is furnished, for example, to the all-important task of setting long-term objectives. Consulting people before major changes take place will also reinforce their commitment and trust.

THINGS TO DO

1. Consider all staff input, no matter how small.
2. Identify "change agents" and encourage them to meet.
3. Form clear plans for change and share your intentions.
4. Tackle resistance to change as early as possible.

IDENTIFYING A
"CHANGE AGENT"

**Is capable of
thinking laterally**

+

**Is driven to improve
and transform**

+

**Is strong and
emotionally in
control**

+

**Thinks forcefully
and independently**

+

**Creates new frames
of reference**

80 Show people how they will gain personally from the changes that you consider are necessary.

MANAGING RESISTANCE

You are likely to encounter varying degrees of resistance from staff when initiating change or revising existing procedures. Do not dismiss or ignore these objections. Some may arise from fear of what lies ahead, so listen to people's objections and, when possible, focus carefully on unwarranted fears in order to reassure staff. Others may arise from reasonable concerns of which you may have been unaware; offer staff the opportunity to explain their worries to you, then clarify how the proposed changes will affect them. Once they feel fully informed, their fears should recede.

QUALITIES FOR CHANGE AGENTS

Organizational change can be blocked by having the wrong people in key roles. Identify members of staff who are open to change – "change agents" – and put them where their enthusiasm for change becomes infectious and allays the fears of other employees. Use them in meetings, allowing them to take a leading role in facilitating the acceptance of change. Place these agents at any level of the organization: they will help you gather feedback on staff morale and reactions to change.

81 Involve many people in producing plans for change.

ASSESSING AND REWARDING

People are employed to generate results for the company.
Their rates of success are intrinsically linked to how they are
directed, reviewed, rewarded, and trusted by management.

EVALUATING PERFORMANCE

*When choosing methods of assessing
your staff's performance, always
make sure that the end result has a positive
effect on motivation and increases people's
sense of self-worth. Realistic targets, positive
feedback, and listening are key factors.*

82 Begin an appraisal
by concentrating
on what a person
has done well.

CULTURAL DIFFERENCES

The British have formal appraisal
systems, but are often lax in
administering them. The French
and Germans set high standards
and expect compliance. In Asia,
group performance is rated
above individual action, whereas
Americans are motivated to
achieve personal targets.

APPRAISING TO MOTIVATE

Regular, one-on-one assessments with your staff
provide an efficient two-way forum in which to
set and review realistic achievement targets,
provide feedback on performance, and listen to
and consider any problems employees may have.
For example, a sales executive may feel that he or
she is underperforming, when in fact sales targets
have been set too high. During the appraisal,
these targets could be reviewed and set at more
realistic levels. Remember that your chosen
methods of assessment must have a positive effect
on people's performance levels and motivation.

JUDGING FAIRLY

An appraisal should leave staff feeling motivated and happy about their work, so make a point of recognizing employees' achievements and unique skills, and offer guidance on ways in which they could improve their performance. Try to avoid using these meetings negatively to criticize and dwell on faults, although do not avoid giving constructive criticism as necessary.

83 If people fail, ask what you can do to help them.

▼ QUALITIES TO APPRAISE
Understand what personal attributes go with successful work behavior, and your judgments and suggestions at appraisals will contribute more effectively to success.

APPRAISING PERSONAL ATTRIBUTES

POSITIVE	NEGATIVE
● Enjoys uncertainty	● Expects certainty
● Asks questions	● Accepts what he or she is told
● Tolerates ambiguity	● Dislikes ambiguity
● Looks for alternatives	● Ignores conflicting evidence
● Is self-critical	● Is impulsive
● Seeks and weighs evidence	● Values "gut feelings"
● Reflects on matters	● Uses "either/or" thinking
● Communicates effectively	● Is unresponsive
● Is willing	● Is reluctant to take on new tasks
● Gets on well with other staff	● Is unpopular
● Uses initiative	● Is not proactive
● Can work unsupervised	● Requires constant supervision
● Is flexible	● Is not adaptable

DEALING WITH UNDERACHIEVEMENT

If objectives are not achieved, ask three key questions (right), and avoid accepting excuses for the answers. You want to find out exactly why the person failed to meet the objectives to prevent it happening again. People regret underachieving, so agree objectives with them that are fair but reasonably stretching. Remember that what seems daunting often proves to be surprisingly easy.

QUESTIONS TO ASK YOURSELF

Q Was the situation understood but the objective too difficult?

Q Was the situation misunderstood or was the objective inappropriate?

Q Was the failure to meet the objective entirely due to causes within the person's control?

PROMOTING STAFF

Giving people new or better jobs shows that you recognize their achievements and encourages them to achieve further success. Rewarding exceptional performance also inspires colleagues to improve their contribution in the workplace.

84 Encourage people to set their own high targets for performance.

▲ **WILL DO – CAN DO**
The employee who shows the standard of behavior that you should always expect is a perfect candidate for promotion.

▲ **WILL DO – CAN'T DO**
The willing employee who experiences difficulties should respond positively to training and encouragement.

▲ **WON'T DO – CAN DO**
The unmotivated person is in danger of losing her job unless motivation can be raised.

▲ **WON'T DO – CAN'T DO**
The incompetent employee who is unwilling to improve should obviously not be retained.

CHOOSING STAFF FOR PROMOTION

A simple, effective way to promote people focuses on two main aspects. Are they able to do the work required? Are they willing to do the work? There are four possible combinations of staff attitude and ability. The willing and able person is the only one you should consider for promotion. At the other extreme, somebody who is neither able nor willing has no place in the organization, let alone on the promotion ladder. The people in-between, who are lacking in either motivation or ability, pose the real challenge to their managers. Motivating an unmotivated person is far more difficult than training a willing individual to perform better. The prospect of promotion, however, may push the unwilling person into trying harder.

THINGS TO DO

1. Prepare a clear and accurate job description.
2. Promote the person who best fits the job description, regardless of age.
3. Seek to promote an employee with a "will do – can do" attitude.
4. If there were other candidates, let them know why they were unsuccessful.
5. Ensure other staff members know the reasons why an employee was promoted.

PROMOTING THE RIGHT PEOPLE

In a traditional, hierarchical system, age comes before ability when people are selected for promotion. However, the diversity of skills in the modern workplace, and people's different aptitudes for them, means that this system is no longer appropriate. Avoid making promotions just because a person was successful in one job: they may not be suited to another. Others whose skills are more suited to the job may feel aggrieved, and the person being promoted will feel insecure. To get the best-qualified person for the job, start with an accurate job specification, and then match the skills and characteristics of the person to the job requirements. Let others know why you have chosen that particular person.

HANDLING DISMISSALS

Job losses are always traumatic and need to be handled sensitively. Whether dismissals are due to redundancies or individual performance problems, once you have made the decision to dismiss someone, implement it quickly. Delaying bad news is always counterproductive: rumors circulate and create anxiety. Set out the facts clearly in all cases of demotion or job loss, so that those affected can understand why the decisions need to be taken. Prepare yourself by considering objections, so that you can deal with them calmly. Be tactful and sympathetic, and as generous as possible with severance payment. In some cases you might consider counseling for those affected. You want those leaving to feel that they have been treated as fairly as possible, and you want to sustain the highest possible morale among your remaining staff.

85 Dismiss only as a last resort, and never fire just to set an example.

86 Be as generous as possible with all severance payments.

TURNING FAILURE INTO SUCCESS

When somebody fails on a project, always consider whether the failure can be turned into a success. Satisfy yourself that you will not be wasting time and money. Then, if there is a reasonable chance of saving the project and the person, take it.

87 Think before you give up on people or plans – giving up is irreversible.

ASSESSING FAILURE

Sometimes an employee does not complete a project successfully. Analyze these failures carefully. Perhaps you or the employee did not have all the necessary information or made false assumptions. Alternatively, if the assumptions were correct, they may have been invalidated by bad execution in which case, identify the mistakes and find out why they were made. The key question is whether, given the results of your research, you would assign another, similar project to the same person. Your answer will determine how best to deal with the employee so as to prevent future failures.

▼ DISCUSSING PROBLEMS AT SOURCE
If an employee has failed on a particular project, you need to discuss the failure with them in detail. If the failure was due to a misunderstanding, for example, the project may be resurrected.

88 Consider cutting your losses rather than carrying on in vague hope.

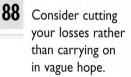

IMPROVING PERFORMANCE

To improve the productivity of an employee who is not performing to the required standard, first consider the factors responsible for this failure. If the person is lacking skills, arrange appropriate training immediately. For minor reasons, such as time-wasting, a verbal warning should be enough. If the reasons are more complex, such as chronic demotivation, consider a plan of action to measure improvement in their performance over a given period. Reassess the situation at the end of this time, and discuss the progress made.

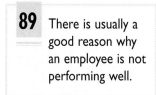

89 There is usually a good reason why an employee is not performing well.

DEALING WITH POOR PERFORMANCE

FAILURE FACTORS	REMEDIAL ACTION
DEMOTIVATION Lacks motivation and energy to improve.	● Tackle the problem immediately. ● Find out possible reasons for drop in motivation. ● Base the improvement plan on a schedule of achievement.
LACK OF SKILLS Cannot cope with the technical demands of the job.	● Find out exactly which skills the employee is lacking. ● Arrange training sessions as soon as possible. ● Assign a person with more appropriate skills to the task.
PROCRASTINATION Finds excuses for not getting on with work.	● Break down the job into more manageable stages. ● Do not let the procrastinator overestimate the time required. ● If necessary, provide hands-on help to get the job started.
ABSENTEEISM Avoids work and dodges responsibility.	● Sternly emphasize the negative effects of absenteeism. ● Ensure that the employee feels an important part of a team. ● Consider if more flexible hours would reduce the problem.
HABITUAL LATENESS Is invariably late and always has an excuse.	● Let it be known that you are not interested in excuses. ● Try a counseling approach before disciplining the employee. ● See if peer pressure from other team members helps.
PERSONAL PROBLEMS Lets personal worries affect work.	● Concentrate on a person's performance, not their problems. ● Consider giving sick leave or reassigning duties. ● If necessary, advise the employee to seek professional help.

REMUNERATING EFFECTIVELY

The way you pay people forms an essential foundation for effective people management. Money is by no means the only motivator of people, but too little money demotivates powerfully, and financial reward remains a strong incentive.

90 Keep basic pay below top rates – use bonuses to give top incomes.

PAYING THE BASICS

The key question for pricing goods – "How much is the market prepared to pay?" – applies just as strongly to remuneration. Ask yourself what level of basic wages and salaries will attract, retain, and motivate people of the caliber that you require. Large companies take pains to discover competitive levels for basic pay, so that they can aim toward the upper limits for their industry. But you should not be concerned only with comparability. You want exceptional results, not comparable performance. Exceptional productivity will more than cover the extra pay. People want to feel fairly rewarded – but they naturally prefer to be rewarded very well.

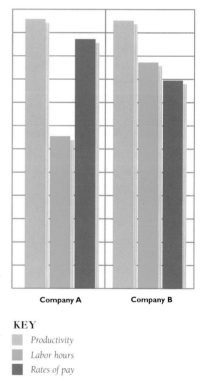

Company A   **Company B**

KEY
- Productivity
- Labor hours
- Rates of pay

INCREASING PAY WITH ▶ BETTER PRODUCTIVITY
Higher levels of efficiency allow you to pay your staff more. Even with fewer labor hours, company A managed to achieve the same level of productivity as company B, making higher rates of pay possible. Company A reached its productivity target thanks to the commitment and motivation of its staff.

PAYING BY RESULTS

The simplest form of payment by results (PBR) is piecework – the employee gets a fixed sum for each unit produced. In theory, this gives the employee the best incentive to maximize output. In fact, employees tend to put a ceiling on their earnings and thus on their effort, so this system has largely disappeared (especially now that more workers are in the information or service industries where piecework cannot be applied). The same principle – more pay for more production – still exists, however, in many forms. In sales, for example, commission can make up a very large proportion of total pay. In many cases, though, the PBR share of remuneration may be less than is necessary to add any real incentive – perhaps as low as five percent. Constantly revise any kind of PBR system that you are involved with to ensure that you are not overpaying for output or getting less output than you require.

TEST YOUR PAYMENT KNOWLEDGE

Answer True or False to the following propositions:
1. Wages and associated expenses determine the cost of labor.
2. The cost of labor determines how competitive your business is.
3. The main way to motivate people is to give financial incentives.
4. The primary incentive for most people at work is money.

(None of these propositions is true.)

91 Always involve employees in pay scale revisions.

92 Make it clear that extra pay is for special achievement.

93 Let team members decide how the team's bonus payment is divided.

GIVING BONUSES

Regard bonus payments as ways for the employee to share in the company's success – not as incentives. Avoid giving all employees an automatic 13 months' pay: they will come to take the annual bonus for granted as part of their basic income. Bonus programs can operate at any or all of three levels: company, team, and individual. Ideally, if the company does well, the individual gets a percentage addition to pay, and the same principle applies if his or her team (maybe a whole division) exceeds its targets. A bonus element tied to individual achievement alone must be reasonably large to be valued. Note the phrase "exceeds its targets": do not pay extra for what has been accepted as a sensible objective.

USING INCENTIVES

Non-cash incentives and fringe benefits can have a powerful influence on attitudes, which should in turn improve results. You can give employees the greatest incentive, however, by imparting a sense of ownership in the organization.

94 Use stock options to reward people for contributing to team success.

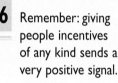

95 Surprise people with gifts they do not expect.

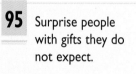

96 Remember: giving people incentives of any kind sends a very positive signal.

SHARING THE SHARES

An employee who sees his or her efforts rewarded in company stock will, in theory, identify with the company, be committed to its success, and perform more effectively. In reality, it may be hard to tell whether the company's success is due to employees owning stock, or whether the success itself has led the company to issue shares. It is also difficult to know whether employees would have performed less effectively if no shares had changed hands. However, by giving people a stake in the company, you are making a highly positive statement about them, which encourages them to feel positive in return.

GIVING GIFTS

Expected remuneration has less impact than the unexpected. Even generous pay raises are taken for granted after a while, as salary aspirations increase accordingly. A far smaller "payment" – in the form of a gift – has a disproportionate worth in the eyes of the recipient. An employee could use a cash award to buy a gift (perhaps a weekend trip), but that provides less satisfaction than a payment in kind from you as reward for work well done. Presents are also a cost-effective method of motivating staff when cash is short or when competition does not allow an increase in pay.

QUESTIONS TO ASK YOURSELF

Q Have I ensured that rewards I have given are what people really want?

Q Am I acting to align the staff's interests with the goals and needs of the organization?

Q Do I always reward achievement and ability in preference to seniority?

Q Have I examined all possible ways of rewarding my staff?

OPTIMIZING BENEFITS

Fringe benefits have become much less effective financially in many countries because of tax changes. Good pension plans, however, have become more attractive wherever state-funded provision has fallen. The same applies to medical insurance – the knowledge that the company cares for its people in sickness, health, and old age is a basic yet very powerful factor. Other benefits, such as company cars, paternity leave, education, and sabbaticals, improve the quality of people's lives. Electronic devices, from mobile telephones to computers, directly benefit the company, but the individual also gains personally from their availability. Ultimately, loyal and happy employees tend to work harder, leading to increased overall productivity.

▼ **BENEFIT PACKAGES**
Non-cash incentives, such as vacations, personal gifts, company cars, private medical insurance, help with children's education and care, and other benefits can greatly improve the way employees view and relate to the organization.

97 Make all welfare provisions as generous as possible.

98 Abolish status symbols that act in a divisive, "them and us" way.

ENDOWING STATUS

The modern company, with its flat structure, horizontal management, and open style, avoids status symbols that are divisive and counter-productive. Reserved parking places and separate dining rooms are rightly shunned. However, important-sounding job titles are an easy and economical way of providing recognition and psychological satisfaction. Moreover, outsiders like to deal with important people (although there is an obvious limit to the number of directors and vicepresidents you can appoint). Management can also confer status on those chosen to represent the company at prestigious events, such as conferences and key negotiations.

CREATING PARTNERSHIPS

W*hen people feel that their own success and that of the company are linked, they will be motivated to give their personal best for the good of all. Value the opinions of staff as partners in the company, and treat them with the care you give clients.*

99 Encourage people to work together as partners who help each other.

WORKERS AS PARTNERS

If a partnership is to work, you must treat employees like partners. Wherever possible, involve your staff in processes like decision-making and problem-solving to foster feelings of involvement and equality. Build a sense of community by providing opportunities to see how other departments within the organization operate. This will help everyone to relate to the company as a whole, and to understand the impact of their own contribution to its success. A shared vision is the strongest factor in the employee and organization partnership.

101 Make sure you let people know all the key facts about the business.

DO'S AND DON'TS

✔ Do enable your staff to understand the business.

✔ Do involve staff in decision-making.

✔ Do encourage staff to find partners to work with closely.

✘ Don't keep secrets that can safely be shared among staff.

✘ Don't leave staff in any doubt about future organization plans.

✘ Don't treat people as "cogs in a machine."

100 Value all your employees – they deserve the same treatment and respect as your customers.

WORKERS AS CUSTOMERS

Employees are valuable customers, and should be treated as such. They are customers in two senses. First, they rely on management for their livelihoods, and second, they might be potential or actual buyers of the company's goods or services. Look after your own people as carefully as you would your best customers. Happy people who feel valued will outperform those who do not.

CASE STUDY

One of the major problems at Pro-Act Inc., as with many firms, was that customer requests and inquiries were not passed on from department to department. The management felt that valuable feedback from the sales engineers' customer visits was being wasted, but was unsure how to resolve the matter. As part of a quality improvement exercise the issue was passed over to the engineers themselves for study and resolution. The engineers came up with the idea of a toll-free telephone line. If a customer asked them about a product other than the one they were selling, they could dial the free number, and a central desk would see that the inquiry reached the right place and monitor response. Sales increased, management was delighted, and the engineers were proud of their role.

◀ **PROCESSING FEEDBACK**

The case of Pro-Act highlights the significance of employee suggestions and the importance of acting on them. The toll-free telephone line program was adopted permanently and proved to be a major success. By adopting an employee-driven improvement plan, Pro-Act both increased sales (and therefore profits for the company) and raised the morale and sense of partnership and belonging felt by the engineers.

ACTING ON SUGGESTIONS

THANKING PEOPLE ▼

Suggestion programs provide just one way of making your employees feel that they are in partnership with you and the company. Failure to acknowledge or act on suggestions, however, will have a detrimental effect.

Formal suggestion programs are an easy way for you to make your staff feel involved in the company. Employees are usually deeply knowledgeable about the business, and will have valuable ideas about ways in which it could improve operations. Process suggestions and ideas rapidly, and let people know the fate of their suggestion – preferably by a note signed by their most senior manager. The acceptance of ideas is often accompanied by a small bonus. However, it is healthier if people regard improving the business as part of their normal activity, and expect and get warm recognition for their ideas and contribution to the company's success, rather than financial rewards.

Senior manager gives warm thanks for a helpful suggestion

Employee feels part of a winning team

ASSESSING YOUR ABILITY

Your ability to manage people should improve with experience, but many of the basic requirements can be mastered from the beginning of your career. The following questionnaire covers the key elements in getting people to work with you and for you to your mutual satisfaction – and to the benefit of the organization. If your answer is "never", mark Option 1; if it is "always", mark Option 4, and so on. Use your answers to identify the areas that need most improvement.

OPTIONS

1 Never

2 Occasionally

3 Frequently

4 Always

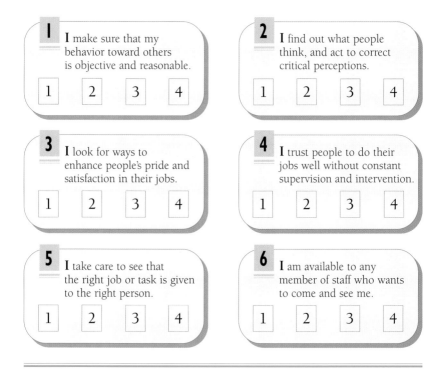

1 I make sure that my behavior toward others is objective and reasonable.

1 2 3 4

2 I find out what people think, and act to correct critical perceptions.

1 2 3 4

3 I look for ways to enhance people's pride and satisfaction in their jobs.

1 2 3 4

4 I trust people to do their jobs well without constant supervision and intervention.

1 2 3 4

5 I take care to see that the right job or task is given to the right person.

1 2 3 4

6 I am available to any member of staff who wants to come and see me.

1 2 3 4

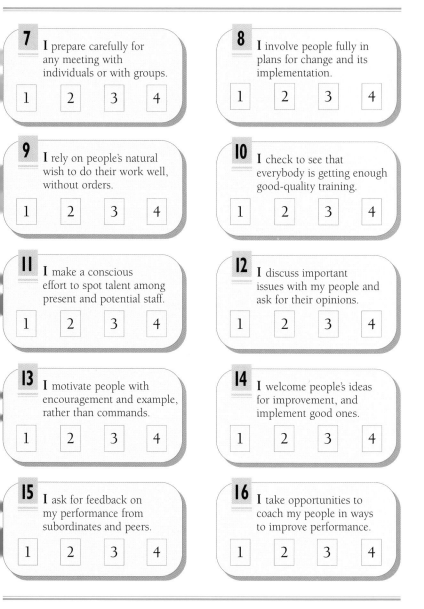

7 I prepare carefully for any meeting with individuals or with groups.

1 | 2 | 3 | 4

8 I involve people fully in plans for change and its implementation.

1 | 2 | 3 | 4

9 I rely on people's natural wish to do their work well, without orders.

1 | 2 | 3 | 4

10 I check to see that everybody is getting enough good-quality training.

1 | 2 | 3 | 4

11 I make a conscious effort to spot talent among present and potential staff.

1 | 2 | 3 | 4

12 I discuss important issues with my people and ask for their opinions.

1 | 2 | 3 | 4

13 I motivate people with encouragement and example, rather than commands.

1 | 2 | 3 | 4

14 I welcome people's ideas for improvement, and implement good ones.

1 | 2 | 3 | 4

15 I ask for feedback on my performance from subordinates and peers.

1 | 2 | 3 | 4

16 I take opportunities to coach my people in ways to improve performance.

1 | 2 | 3 | 4

17 I give people the chance to demonstrate their management abilities.

| 1 | 2 | 3 | 4 |

18 I set high standards and insist that those standards are met.

| 1 | 2 | 3 | 4 |

19 I give people clear responsibility for a task that they can "own."

| 1 | 2 | 3 | 4 |

20 I form small groups or teams to tackle specific projects or needs.

| 1 | 2 | 3 | 4 |

21 I ask everybody in the team to come to a discussion with one or two new ideas.

| 1 | 2 | 3 | 4 |

22 I deal with people's personal problems swiftly and sympathetically.

| 1 | 2 | 3 | 4 |

23 I am prepared to listen to others and change my mind on issues.

| 1 | 2 | 3 | 4 |

24 I keep anger and other negative emotions out of my decisions and actions.

| 1 | 2 | 3 | 4 |

25 I try to understand the opposing point of view in cases of conflict.

| 1 | 2 | 3 | 4 |

26 I resolve interpersonal disputes quickly and without prejudice.

| 1 | 2 | 3 | 4 |

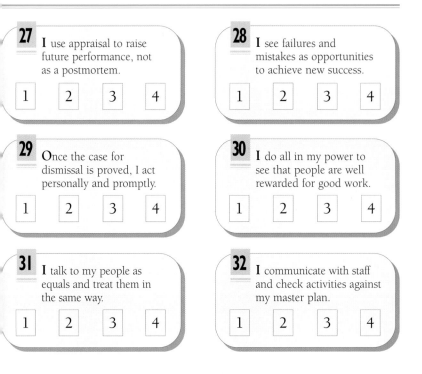

27 I use appraisal to raise future performance, not as a postmortem.

1   2   3   4

28 I see failures and mistakes as opportunities to achieve new success.

1   2   3   4

29 Once the case for dismissal is proved, I act personally and promptly.

1   2   3   4

30 I do all in my power to see that people are well rewarded for good work.

1   2   3   4

31 I talk to my people as equals and treat them in the same way.

1   2   3   4

32 I communicate with staff and check activities against my master plan.

1   2   3   4

ANALYSIS

Now that you have completed the self-assessment, add up the scores and check your performance by referring to the corresponding evaluations:

32–63: You are clearly having difficulties in dealing with people. The problems must be having a noticeable and unwelcome effect on your performance as well as your working environment. It is important to take action at once, probably with help from others, to begin badly needed improvement.

64–95: You are reasonably good with people but, in human relations at work, good is not enough. Use the questionnaire to identify your weaker areas, and work on them to get better results from yourself and others.

96–128: You should be pleased with your success with people, but remember that dealing with them is an ongoing process that can always be improved on.

INDEX

A

ability:
nurturing talent, 32–33
spotting, 34
achievement, and motivation, 36
action learning, 31
activity training, 25
analytical skills, 26
anger, defusing negative
emotions, 47
anxiety, defusing negative
emotions, 47
appraisal systems, 54–55
appropriate behavior, 7
Asia, cultural differences, 54
assessments:
of failure, 58
of performance, 54–55
autonomy, and motivation, 36

B

behavior, understanding, 6–7
benefits, as incentives, 63
body language, 11
bonus payments, 21, 61
boredom, 20, 43
bureaucracy, 15

C

"can-do" atmosphere, 21
career development, 35
cells, working in, 26
change, managing, 52–53
"change agents", 52, 53
closed minds, opening, 44–45
cooperation, 7
coaching, 28
collective problems, 48–49
commission, 61
commitment, 18–21
communication, 14–17
cutting bureaucracy, 15
eliminating fear, 13
encouraging contact, 14
"grapevine", 17
office politics, 43
one-to-one meetings, 16
team meetings, 17

using different media, 16
competence, and motivation, 36
complaints, personal difficulties,
50
computers:
communication via, 16
training in, 27
confidence building, 12–13
conflicts:
collective problems, 48–49
dealing with, 46–47
personal difficulties, 50
constructive behavior, 6, 7
consultation, 23
counselors, 29, 57
creativity, 43, 44
criticism, reactions to, 6
cultural differences:
appraisal systems, 54
personal difficulties, 51
teaching, 31
customers, workers as, 64

D

decentralized organizations,
communication, 15
decision-making:
delegation, 37
involving staff, 52
workers as partners, 64
delegation, 37
deployment policy, 41
discipline, 22
dismissal, 57
disputes:
collective problems, 48–49
dealing with, 46–47
personal difficulties, 50
dissatisfaction, 8, 19

E

email, 16, 27
electronic media, 16
emotions:
defusing negative emotions, 47
emotional needs, 19
natural behavior, 6
entrepreneurial organizations,
communication, 15

excellence, rewarding, 21
experience, learning by, 39
expertise, and motivation, 36

F

failure, dealing with, 58–59
fear, eliminating, 13
financial incentives, 21, 60–61
flexibility, 23, 41
France, cultural differences, 54
fringe benefits, 63

G

gender issues, 51
Germany, cultural differences, 31,
51, 54
gifts, 62
"grapevine", 17
guiding others, 28–29
guilt, defusing negative emotions,
47

H

harassment, 51
"heroes", 21
"hierarchy of needs", 8

I

ideas:
accepting, 44
ideas meetings, 39
improvement themes, deployment
policy, 41
incentives:
and commitment, 21
financial, 61
fringe benefits, 63
stock options, 62
insecurity, reducing, 12–13
insurance, medical, 63
intellectual needs, 19
Intranets, 27

J K L

Japan, cultural differences, 31, 51
job descriptions, and promotion, 57
job titles, as incentive, 63
job loss, 57
Kami, Michael J., 33

Leadership:
  role models, 30
  trust and commitment, 18
learning by experience, 39
listening, 10–11

M
McGregor, Douglas, 22
magazines, in-house, 16
managerial training, 25
manufacturing cells, 26
market-oriented organizations,
  communication, 15
Maslow, Abraham, 8
matrix organizations,
  communication, 15
media, communication, 16
medical insurance, 63
meetings:
  ideas meetings, 39
  one-to-one meetings, 16
  team meetings, 17
membership, and motivation, 36
mentors, 29
mind-sets, changing, 45
morale:
  of group, 40
  handling dismissals, 57
motivation, 36–37
  appraisal systems, 54
  coaching and, 28
  and commitment, 20
  loss of, 42
  and promotion, 56
multi-skilling, 26
multi-tasking, 23

N
natural behavior, 6, 7
needs:
  emotional, 19
  intellectual, 19
  psychological, 19
  understanding, 8–9
negative emotions, 47
newsletters, in-house, 16
nonconformist employees, 33
"Not Invented Here" (NIH)
  syndrome, 44

O
office politics, 43
one-to-one meetings, 16
open-plan offices, 14
outsourcing, 41

P
participation, 13
partnerships, creating, 64–65
payment by results (PBR), 61
peer respect, and motivation, 36
pension plans, 63
people-based organizations,
  communication, 15
performance:
  assessment of, 54–55
  improving, 38–39, 59
personal development, 20,
  24–39, 56
personal difficulties, 50–51
personality:
  personality clashes, 50
  "talented gorillas", 33
piecework, 61
practical abilities, 35
praise, 12, 21
pressure, coping with, 35
pride in work, 9
productivity:
  improving, 59
  and salary levels, 60
professional training, 25
promotion, 56–57
  choosing staff for, 56–57
  facilitating, 34, 35
  planning succession, 32
psychological needs, 19

Q
quality:
  Quality Improvement Projects
    (QIP), 43
  and responsibility, 40
  Total Quality Management
    (TQM), 38
  training, 25

R
recognition, and motivation, 36
remuneration see financial
  incentives
resistance to change, 53
responsibility, 23, 40
rewards:
  and commitment, 21
  gifts, 62
  and motivation, 56
risk-taking, 45
role models, teaching by example,
  30

S
salaries, 21, 60–61, 62
self-confidence, 7
  building, 12–13
  and motivation, 36
self-fulfillment, 36
self-management, 37
self-respect, 36
sexual harassment, 51
skills:
  improving performance, 59
  management qualities, 34–35
  multi-skilling, 26
  and promotion, 57
  sharing, 31
  training, 25, 26–27
stock options, 21, 62
status symbols, 63
strategy, and motivation, 36
subordinates, promotion, 32
succession, planning, 32
suggestion schemes, 65
supervisors, quality control, 40

T
talent, nurturing, 32–33
teaching by example, 30–31
teams:
  conflict within, 48
  meetings, 17
  morale, 40
  sharing skills, 31
  team spirit, 42
technical training, 25
technology, computer training, 27
Theory X management, 22
Theory Y management, 22
thinking skills, 26
Total Quality Management
  (TQM), 38
training, 24–25
  and commitment, 20
  computer literacy, 27
  and promotion, 35
trust, 18

UW
unconventional employees, 33
underachievement, dealing with,
  55
unions, 48, 49
United States, cultural differences,
  31, 51, 54
Web sites, 16

ACKNOWLEDGMENTS

AUTHOR'S ACKNOWLEDGMENTS

This book owes its existence to the perceptive inspiration of Stephanie Jackson and Nigel Duffield at Dorling Kindersley; and I owe more than I can say to the expertise and enthusiasm of Jane Simmonds and all the editorial and design staff who worked on the project. I am also greatly indebted to the many colleagues, friends, and other management luminaries on whose wisdom and information I have drawn.

PUBLISHER'S ACKNOWLEDGMENTS

Dorling Kindersley would like to thank the following for their help and participation in producing this book:

Editorial Alison Bolus, Michael Downey, Nicola Munro, Sean O'Connor, Jane Simmonds, Sylvia Tombesi-Walton; **Indexer** Hilary Bird.

Design Pauline Clarke, Jamie Hanson, Nigel Morris, Tish Mills, Laura Watson.

DTP assistance Rob Campbell.

Photography Steve Gorton; **Photography assistance** Nici Harper, Andy Komorowski.

Models Phil Argent, Angela Cameron, Kuo Kang Chen, Patrick Dobbs, Carole Evans, Vosjava Fahkro, John Gillard, Ben Glickman, Richard Hill, Cornell John, Janey Madlani, Maggie Mant, Sotiris Meliomis, Karen Murray, Mary Jane Robinson, Lois Sharland, Lynne Staff, Peter Taylor, Suki Tan, Ann Winterborn, Gilbert Wu, Wendy Yun.

Makeup Debbie Finlow, Janice Tee.

Suppliers Austin Reed, Bally, Church & Co., Clark Davis & Co. Ltd, Compaq, David Clulow Opticians, Geiger Brickel, Elonex, Escada, Filofax, Gateway 2000, Moss Bros, Mucci Bags, Staverton. With thanks to Tony Ash at Geiger Brickel (Office Furniture) and Carron Williams at Bally (Shoes).

Picture research Andy Sansom; **Picture library assistance** Sue Hadley, Rachel Hilford, Denise O'Brien, Melanie Simmonds.

PICTURE CREDITS

Key: *a* above, *b* bottom, *c* centre, *l* left, *r* right, *t* top
Telegraph Colour Library Benelux Press 14, Elke Hebber 63, Terry McCormick 58, Ed Taylor 4, front jacket *tl*; **Tony Stone Images** Walter Hodges 26, 48, Antonio Mo 42, Stephen Peters 6.

AUTHOR'S BIOGRAPHY

Robert Heller is a leading authority in the world of management consulting and was the founding editor of Britain's top management magazine, *Management Today*. He is much in demand as a conference speaker in Europe, North and South America, and the Far East. As editorial director of Haymarket Publishing Group, Robert Heller supervised the launch of several highly successful magazines such as *Campaign*, *Computing*, and *Accountancy Age*. His many acclaimed – and worldwide best-selling – books include *The Naked Manager*, *Culture Shock*, *The Age of the Common Millionaire*, *The Way to Win* (with Will Carling), *The Complete Guide to Modern Management*, and *In Search of European Excellence*. Robert Heller has also written a number of earlier books in the Dorling Kindersley *Essential Managers* series.